Searchlight BOOKS™

How Does Your Body Work?

Your
Digestive System

Rebecca L. Johnson

Lerner Publications Company
Minneapolis

For R & T, always there

Lerner Publications Company
A division of Lerner Publishing Group, Inc.
241 First Avenue North
Minneapolis, MN 55401 U.S.A.

Website address: www.lernerbooks.com

Library of Congress Cataloging-in-Publication Data

Johnson, Rebecca L.
    Your digestive system / by Rebecca L. Johnson.
        p.   cm. — (Searchlight books™—how does your body work?)
    Includes index.
    ISBN 978–0–7613–7448–0 (lib. bdg. : alk. paper)
    1. Digestion—Juvenile literature. 2. Gastrointestinal system—Physiology—Juvenile literature. I. Title.
QP145.J65 2013
612.3—dc23   2011034265

Manufactured in the United States of America
1 – CG – 7/15/12

Contents

Chapter 1

FUEL FOR LIFE

Mmmm! There's fresh, hot pizza! You are so hungry. Your stomach is growling. You take a big bite. Cheese, crust, and sauce mix together in your mouth. Is pizza your favorite food? Maybe it's pudding, peaches, or pot roast. There are thousands of foods. Think of all the kinds of food you eat.

When you're hungry, pizza tastes great! What does your stomach do when you're hungry?

Food is more than yummy tastes or crunchy mouthfuls. Food is fuel. It gives your body and your mind energy. Good food keeps you healthy and strong.

Eating good food keeps you strong and active.

Changing Food to Nutrients

But food must be changed before your body can use it. Your body must digest it first.

   When you digest food, it is broken down into nutrients. Nutrients feed your body and keep it working well.

EATING GOOD FOOD ALSO
HELPS YOU THINK.

Your body is made up of billions of cells. Cells are like tiny building blocks. They work together to form every part of you. Your skin, bones, and muscles are made of cells. Cells make up your eyes, heart, and all of your other organs too.

Your body uses nutrients to fix damaged cells. It uses nutrients to make new cells. It uses nutrients for energy too. That energy gives you the power to live and grow.

Nutrients give cells what they need to grow, divide, and work. This cell is about to split into two cells.

Chapter 2

IN YOUR MOUTH

Food is digested in your digestive system. A system is a way of doing things. Your digestive system is like a long tube. It has a few bulges here and there. The tube twists and turns all the way through your body.

You start to take a bite of your pizza. Where will it go?

A Long Trip

Remember that bite of pizza? It is about to enter your digestive system. It has a long trip ahead. So let's follow that food!

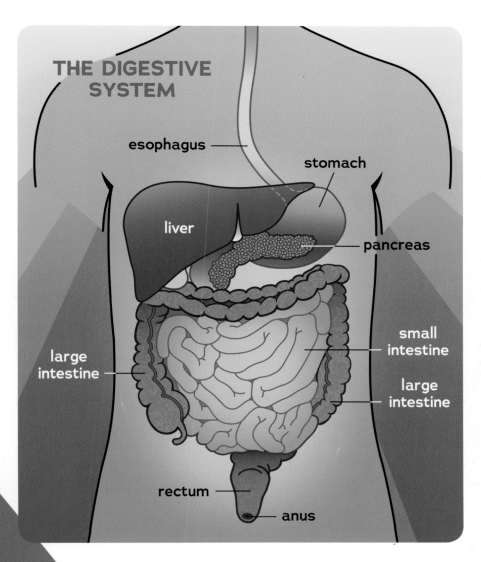

THE DIGESTIVE SYSTEM

esophagus

stomach

liver

pancreas

large intestine

small intestine

large intestine

rectum

anus

Your Teeth

As you chew, your teeth break up the pizza. You chew it into smaller and smaller pieces.

You have several kinds of teeth in your mouth. They have different shapes. Each kind of tooth works on food in a different way. Your front teeth bite and tear your food. And your back teeth grind your food.

Your front teeth have sharp edges. They are good for biting off a chunk of food.

Saliva

As you chew, a liquid mixes with the food in your mouth. This watery liquid is called saliva. Saliva is one kind of digestive juice. Digestive juices help break down food in your digestive system.

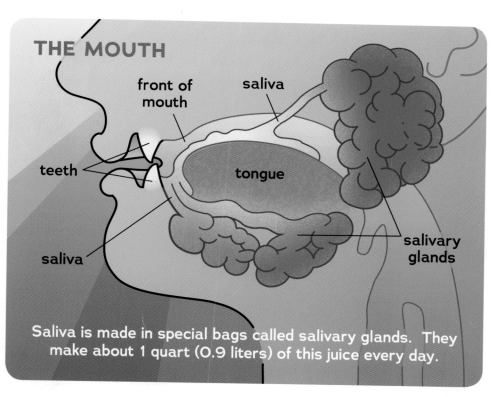

THE MOUTH

front of mouth

saliva

teeth

tongue

saliva

salivary glands

Saliva is made in special bags called salivary glands. They make about 1 quart (0.9 liters) of this juice every day.

Your Tongue

Chewed food gets soft and slimy as it mixes with saliva. Your tongue shapes the food into a lump. When you are ready to swallow, your tongue pushes the lump. The lump moves to the back of your mouth, where your throat begins.

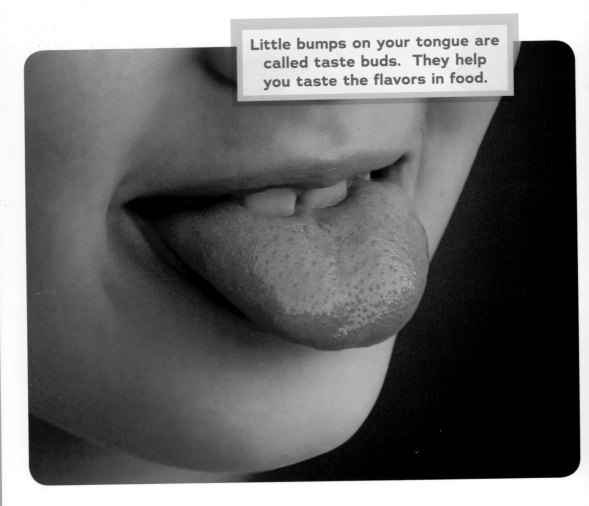

Little bumps on your tongue are called taste buds. They help you taste the flavors in food.

Your Esophagus and Your Trachea

Your throat sits at the top of two tubes. The esophagus is the tube that leads to your stomach. The other tube is the trachea. It leads to your lungs.

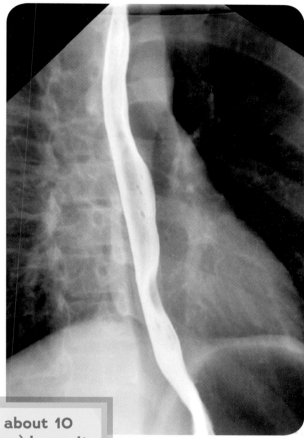

Your esophagus is about 10 inches (25 centimeters) long. It connects your mouth to your stomach. This X-ray photo shows part of the esophagus.

At the top of your trachea is a little flap of skin. It is called the epiglottis. When you swallow, the epiglottis flops down. It closes the trachea. That way, food doesn't get into your lungs by mistake.

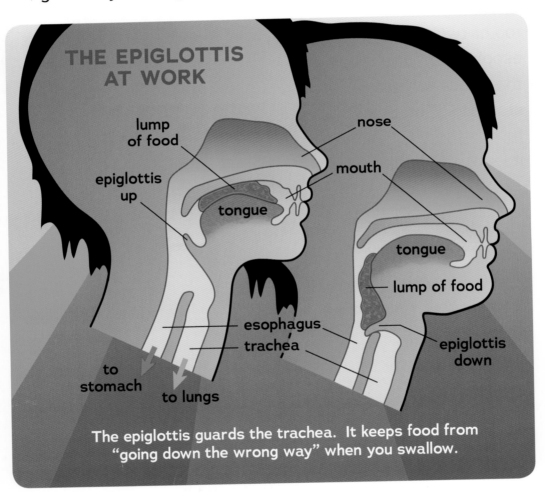

THE EPIGLOTTIS AT WORK

lump of food

epiglottis up

tongue

nose

mouth

tongue

lump of food

esophagus

trachea

to stomach

to lungs

epiglottis down

The epiglottis guards the trachea. It keeps food from "going down the wrong way" when you swallow.

Swallowed food doesn't just fall down the esophagus to your stomach. Muscles are in the wall of the esophagus. The muscles squeeze behind the lump of food. The squeezing pushes the food along. It's like squeezing toothpaste out of a tube.

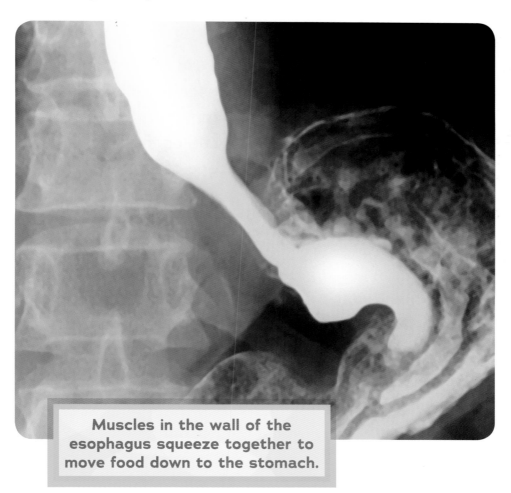

Muscles in the wall of the esophagus squeeze together to move food down to the stomach.

The ring of muscles at the bottom of your esophagus opens only when food is coming down. This keeps food that is already in the stomach from moving back up into the esophagus.

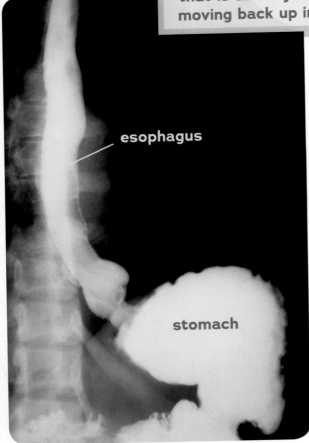

esophagus

stomach

At the bottom of the esophagus is a ring of muscles. The muscles can open and close that end of the esophagus. Most of the time, the ring is tightly closed. But when food comes down the tube, the muscles relax. They let the lump of food move into your stomach.

Chapter 3

IN YOUR STOMACH

Digestion continues when food reaches your stomach. The stomach has a stretchy wall. The wall is covered with special cells. Some of these cells make digestive juice. The juice continues breaking down the food.

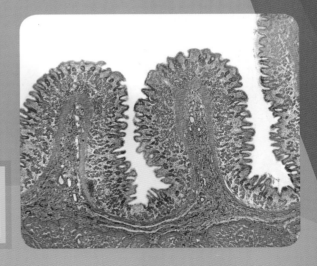

Special cells line the wall of your stomach. What do some of these cells do?

Acid and Mucus

Other stomach cells make acid. Acid is a liquid that softens food. It also kills any germs in the food.

And other cells make slippery, slimy mucus. Mucus coats the food. Mucus also coats the wall of the stomach.

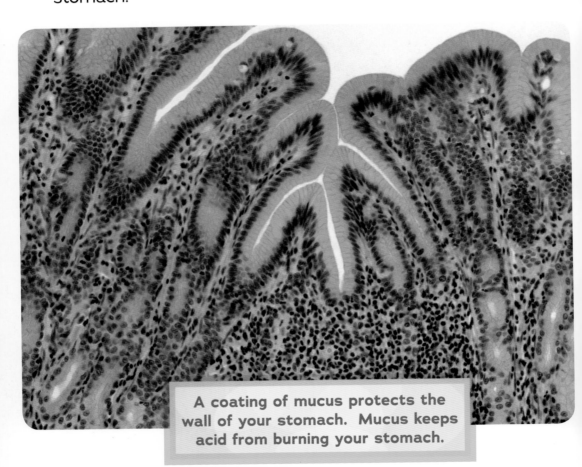

A coating of mucus protects the wall of your stomach. Mucus keeps acid from burning your stomach.

About every twenty seconds, muscles in the stomach wall squeeze. This squeezing mixes the food with digestive juice, acid, and mucus. This mixing goes on for several hours. It turns the pizza you ate into a soupy liquid.

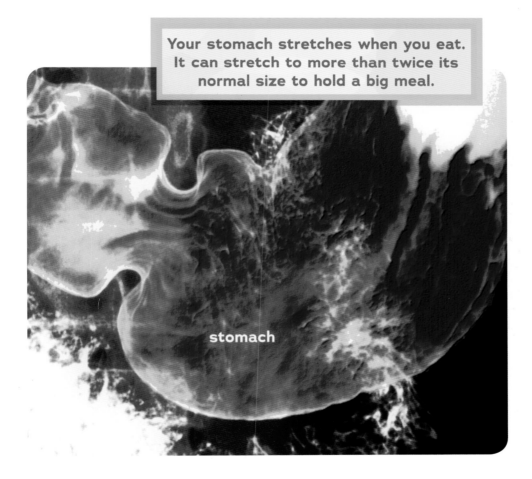

Your stomach stretches when you eat. It can stretch to more than twice its normal size to hold a big meal.

stomach

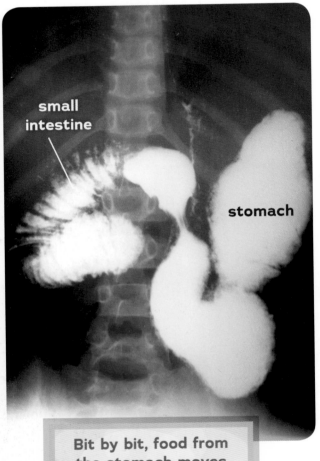

small
intestine

stomach

Bit by bit, food from
the stomach moves
into the small intestine.

At the bottom of the stomach is a small hole. The hole is surrounded by a ring of muscles. Every few minutes, the ring of muscles relaxes. The hole opens. Some of the soupy liquid squirts out of your stomach and into the small intestine.

Chapter 4

TAKING UP NUTRIENTS

Your small intestine is a narrow tube that loops around and around in your belly. It is the longest part of your digestive system. It is about 20 feet (6 meters) long.

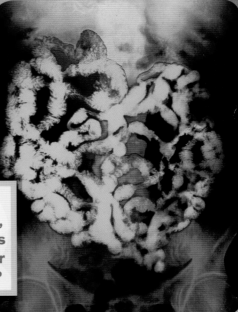

If you could stretch your small intestine out straight, it would be about as long as a school bus. Where in your body is the small intestine?

When food enters the beginning of the small intestine, more digestive juices are added. These juices come from two organs called the pancreas and the liver.

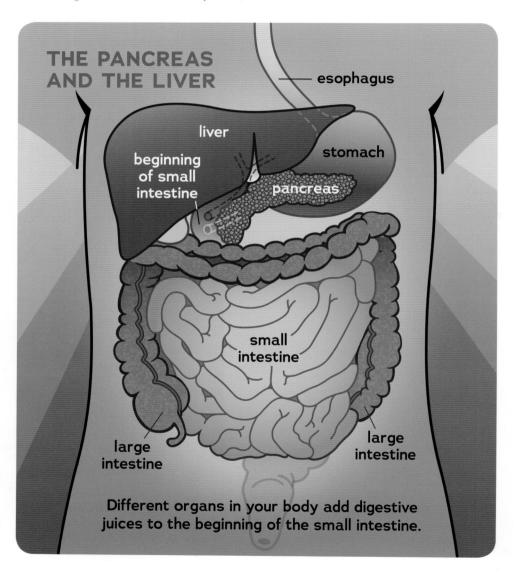

THE PANCREAS AND THE LIVER

esophagus

liver

beginning of small intestine

stomach

pancreas

small intestine

large intestine

large intestine

Different organs in your body add digestive juices to the beginning of the small intestine.

From Pizza to Nutrients

Muscles in the wall of the small intestine squeeze together. They push the food slowly along. More mucus is added to keep the food moving smoothly.

Slowly but surely, the digestive juices finish their work. The pizza becomes a mix of nutrients. The nutrients are very small.

This photo was taken with a microscope. It shows tiny bits of digested food that are stuck to the wall of the small intestine.

Villi

The inside surface of the small intestine is covered with millions of tiny bumps. These bumps are called villi. They are shaped like tiny fingers. The walls of the villi are very thin.

Inside the villi are tiny blood vessels. Blood vessels are tubes that carry blood through your body. Nutrients can go through the thin walls of the villi and into your blood.

Millions and millions of bumps called villi cover the inside surface of the small intestine.

The Liver's Work

Blood carries nutrients to the liver. The liver cleans the blood. It strains out nutrients when they arrive. Some nutrients are stored in the liver. They stay there until the body needs them.

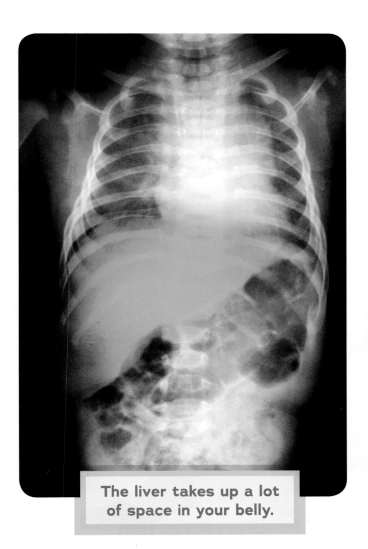

The liver takes up a lot of space in your belly.

Other nutrients leave the liver quickly. Before they go, the liver changes them. It makes the nutrients easier for cells to use. Blood carries these nutrients all around your body. They are delivered to each and every one of your cells.

Nutrients are carried in the blood. The blood delivers nutrients to cells.

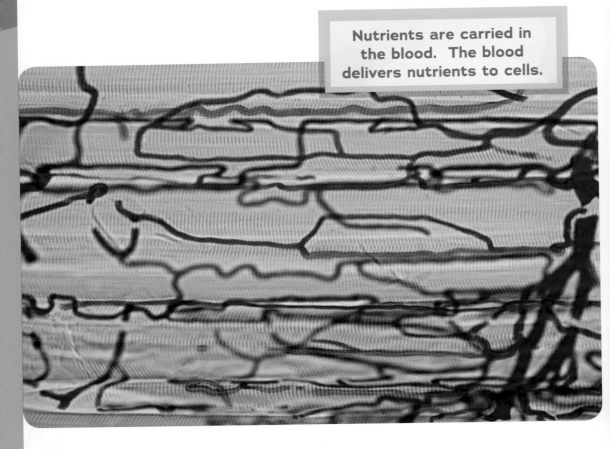

Using Nutrients

Your body uses some nutrients to grow taller. It uses others to build strong bones and teeth. Still other nutrients are used by muscles to help you move.

NUTRIENTS HELP YOU GROW TALL.

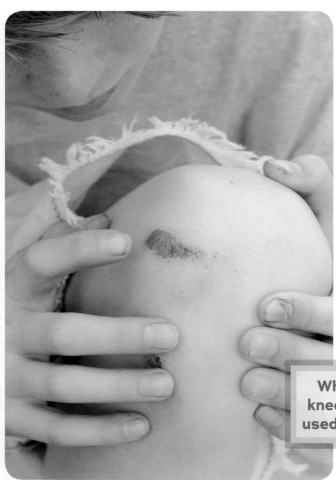

Nutrients are also needed for repairing your body. When you skin your knee, your cells use nutrients to make a scab. The scab covers the wound. Nutrients also help new cells grow to replace the skin that was lost.

When you scrape your knee, some nutrients are used to fix damaged cells.

Chapter 5

GETTING RID OF WASTES

By the time food reaches the end of your small intestine, digestion is finished. Most of the nutrients in your pizza have passed into your blood. All that is left is waste.

The large intestine begins where the small intestine ends. What is left when food reaches the end of your small intestine?

The Large Intestine

Waste moves into the large intestine. The large intestine is the last part of the digestive system. It is wider than the small intestine. But it is only about 5 feet (1.5 m) long. That's about as long as a bicycle.

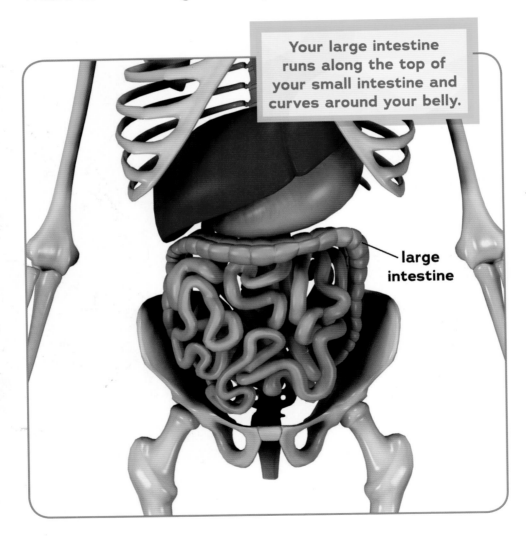

Your large intestine runs along the top of your small intestine and curves around your belly.

large intestine

The large intestine forms a big loop in your belly. It runs up your right side. Then it goes across your middle and down your left side. The last part of the large intestine is the rectum.

The walls of the large intestine are smooth on the inside. There are no villi here.

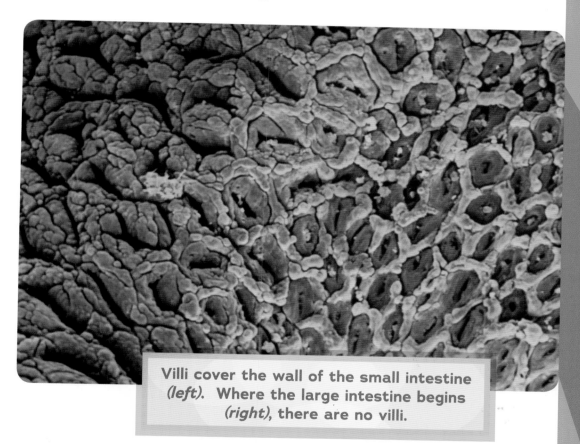

Villi cover the wall of the small intestine *(left)*. Where the large intestine begins *(right)*, there are no villi.

Muscles help push waste through your large intestine. As waste moves along, it loses water. The water goes through the wall of the large intestine. It is used by your cells.

The waste becomes more solid. It is shaped into soft masses called feces.

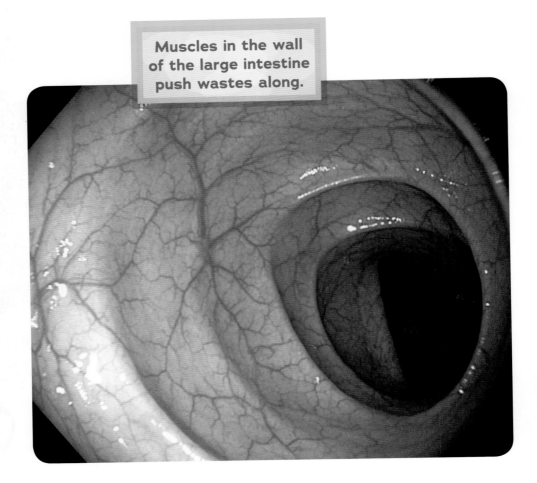

Muscles in the wall of the large intestine push wastes along.

Eventually, feces get to the rectum. There is an opening at the end of the rectum. It is called the anus. Most of the time, the anus is held closed by a ring of muscles. When you have to go to the bathroom, these muscles relax. The feces pass out of your body.

Getting rid of waste is a part of digestion. After you go to the bathroom, it's important to wash your hands.

It takes about twenty-four hours for a meal to move through your digestive system. The exact time depends on the size of your meal. It also depends on the kinds of food you ate.

Once you swallow food, you don't have to think about digestion. You can't control it. It just happens. But you can control what kinds of food you eat. You can control how much you eat.

Eating healthful foods will give your body the nutrients it needs.

Being Food Smart

If you eat too much, you take in more nutrients than your body can use. Some extra nutrients are stored in your body as fat. Too much stored fat is unhealthful.

WHEN YOU'RE HUNGRY FOR SNACKS, HEALTHFUL FOODS WILL GIVE YOUR BODY WHAT IT NEEDS.

If you eat too little, you may not get all the nutrients you need. If you eat only a few kinds of foods, you won't get all the nutrients you need either. Eating well gives you the energy to do the things you want to do. If you feed your body the right fuel, you'll be more likely to be healthy and strong.

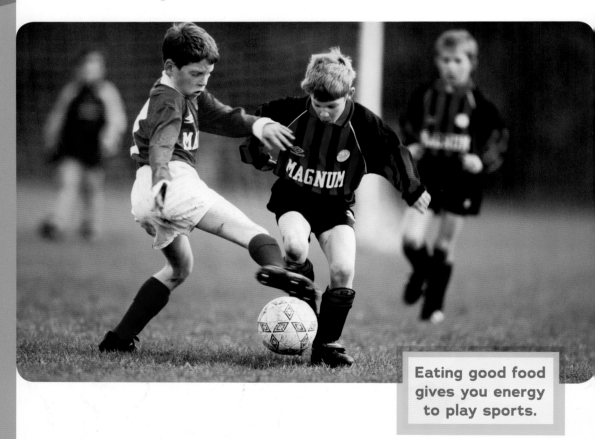

Eating good food gives you energy to play sports.

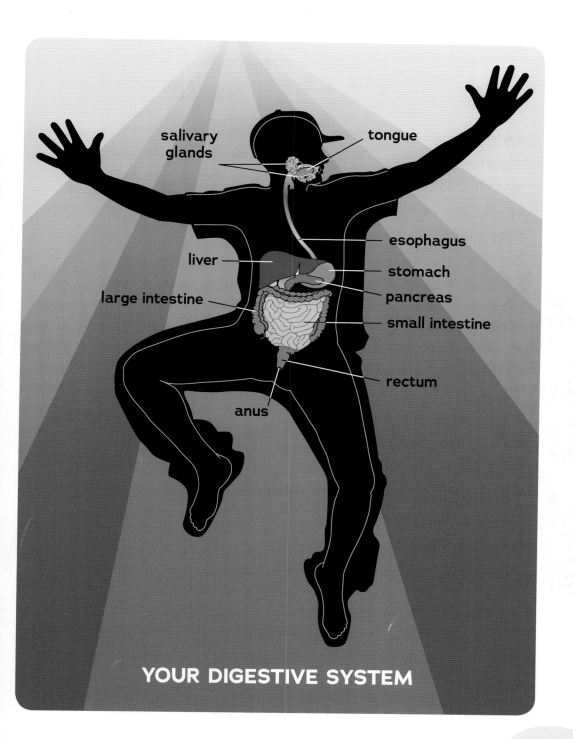

salivary glands

tongue

esophagus

liver

stomach

pancreas

large intestine

small intestine

rectum

anus

YOUR DIGESTIVE SYSTEM

Glossary

acid: liquid made in the stomach that softens food and kills germs in food

digest: to break food down so the body can use it

digestive juice: liquid that helps break food down into smaller, simpler parts

epiglottis: the flap of skin that keeps food out of the lungs

esophagus: the tube that connects the mouth to the stomach

liver: a part of the body that makes digestive juice. It also helps the body use digested food.

mucus: a slimy liquid that covers the walls of the stomach and intestines

nutrients: the parts of food that feed the body and keep it working well

organ: a part of the body that does a particular job. The stomach, the liver, and the heart are organs.

pancreas: a body part that makes digestive juice

rectum: the end of the large intestine

saliva: a liquid in your mouth that helps break down food

trachea: the tube that connects the mouth to the lungs

villi: tiny bumps on the walls of the small intestines

Learn More about the Digestive System

Books

Doeden, Matt. *Eat Right! How You Can Make Good Food Choices*. Minneapolis: Lerner Publications Company, 2009. Read more about being food smart in this fun and useful book.

Donovan, Sandy. *Rumble & Spew: Gross Stuff in Your Stomach and Intestines*. Minneapolis: Millbrook Press, 2010. Do you like to learn about the gross and funny side of science? Then check out this entertaining look at all the icky stuff related to your digestive system.

Simon, Seymour. *Guts: Our Digestive System*. New York: HarperCollins, 2005. Simon explains why it's important to chew your food, how long it takes to digest food, and why a healthful diet is important.

Taylor-Butler, Christine. *The Digestive System*. New York: Children's Press, 2008. This informative title explores the digestive system, digestive disorders, and how doctors examine your digestive system.

Websites

Enchanted Learning: Fruit and Vegetable Activities and Information
http://www.zoomschool.com/themes/fruit.shtml
This website features fun crafts and information related to fruits and vegetables.

IMCPL Kids' Info Guide: Digestive System
http://www.imcpl.org/kids/guides/health/digestivesystem.html
This page from the Indianapolis Marion County Public Library has a list of resources you can use to learn more about the digestive system.

KidsHealth: How the Body Works
http://kidshealth.org/kid/htbw/htbw_main_page.html
Click on the stomach to watch a movie, read articles, and solve a word puzzle about this important part of the digestive system. You can also learn about other body parts, such as the liver and the teeth.

Index

Photo Acknowledgments

The images in this book are used with the permission of: © Hill Street Studios/Blend Images/Getty Images, p. 4; © Purestock/Getty Images, p. 5; © iStockphoto.com/Bart Coenders, p. 6; © David M. Phillips / Photo Researchers, Inc., p. 7; © Aaron Farley/The Image Bank/Getty Images, p. 8; © Laura Westlund/Independent Picture Service, pp. 9, 11, 14, 22, 37; © Radius Images/Getty Images, p. 10; © Science Faction/SuperStock, p. 12; © Living Art Enterprises/Photo Researchers, Inc., p. 13; © Miriam Maslo/Science Photo Library/Getty Images, p. 15; © Ed Reschke/Peter Arnold/Getty Images, p. 16; © Garry DeLong/Photo Researchers, Inc., p. 17; © Steve Gschmeissner/Science Photo Library/Getty Images, pp. 18, 24; © Pasieka/Science Photo Library/Getty Images, p. 19; © MedicImage/Universal Images Group/Getty Images, p. 20; © Barts Hospital/Stone/Getty Images, p. 21; © Biophoto Associates/Photo Researchers, Inc., p. 23; © Camazine Scott/Photo Researchers/Getty Images, p. 25; © Dr. Cecil H. Fox/Photo Researchers/Getty Images, p. 26; © Dana Menussi/The Image Bank/Getty Images, p. 27; © Suzanne Tucker/Shutterstock.com, p. 28; © Medical Body Scans /Photo Researchers, Inc., p. 29; © Friedrich Saurer/Photo Researchers, Inc., p. 30; © Prof. P.M. Motta/Univ. "La Sapienza", Rome/Photo Researchers, Inc., p. 31; © Gastrolab/Photo Researchers, Inc., p. 32; © iStockphoto.com/Nina Shannon, p. 33; © Jose Luis Pelaez Inc/Blend Images/Getty Images, p. 34; © Hannamariah/Shutterstock.com, p. 35; © Chris Cole/The Image Bank/Getty Images, p. 36.

Front cover: © Mads Abildgaard/the Agency Collection/Getty Images.

Main body text set in Adrianna Regular 14/20
Typeface provided by Chank